# 20 Nothing to Something

*Unlock the chains of unfulfilled potential,*
*and manifest the life you want with*
*these six over-spoken but underutilised tools,*
*to ensure you own your 20s.*

## OLAJUMOKE CHAMPION

Grosvenor House
Publishing Limited

This book is published by
Grosvenor House Publishing Ltd
Link House
140 The Broadway, Tolworth, Surrey, KT6 7HT.
www.grosvenorhousepublishing.co.uk

A CIP record for this book
is available from the British Library

ISBN 978-1-83975-669-6

# CONTENTS

# ACKNOWLEDGEMENTS

## 1) My mother

To my beautiful mother who has always stood by my side through thick and thin, who has supported me and helped me to see my right and wrong doings. Even though sometimes I was defiant and hard work, I am grateful to you always and forever for the woman you have helped me to become, as I know how much I have fought to become her.

## 2) My father

It's not every day you meet a man that teaches you from a young age what you do and don't want in a man. Thank you for always reminding me that I'm beautiful and telling me I was destined to defy all odds.

## 3) My family and friends

To my friends and family, for always telling me that I motivate and inspire you; for always being there when I need something or someone to fall back on; for the continuous love that you have shown me. I thank you because not only have you allowed me to have a positive effect on your life, but you encouraged me to push myself and inspire others. I am grateful for your support in helping me find myself, and for seeing the potential in what I can do. You are all most definitely heaven-sent.

## 4) Ex-fiancé turned friend

Just for being you. Our relationship has allowed me to experience personal growth that I would not have experienced had I not been with you. Sometimes life sends you someone to teach you things that you would not otherwise learn. Although I love you for the good, I am also thankful for the bad. You have shown me I'm stronger and more capable than I thought.

# DEDICATION

To anyone who has ever felt disorientated and lost.

To anyone whose heart is/was filled with emptiness and unfulfillment.

To anyone whose goals seem ever so distant.

To anyone searching for love in all the wrong places.

To anyone who does not understand how perfect you are just the way you are.

To anyone who does not understand that imperfection is beauty and life is a continuous journey. Learn not to give up, but to continuously work on self-improvement to enjoy the true journey of life.

To anyone that picks up this book, may you find happiness and success; I am here to remind you that you are worthy and more resilient than you think. Understand that to become the person you want to be, you must first visualise it, then fight daily to become them.

I had to change my habits, my thought process, and my attitude, to become the woman I am today, and I want to share with you the simple lessons that I wish I had learnt earlier, and that helped me become who I have always wanted to be.

You must be dedicated and focused; the journey will not be easy, but I can assure you it will be worth it.

The feeling of unfulfillment used to be a familiar one to me. Although the feeling had been following me around for many years, it only became evident to me by the time I got to university.

What I found interesting is how I was able to live with it for so long without even realising what the feeling really was and how I was supposed to deal with it. The worst part is that I feel like many of us do exactly that: we have that unfamiliar feeling, but instead of trying to work out what it is or why we feel that way, we push it aside to force ourselves to just live with it, hence that particular feeling seems to reoccur.

If you asked people to describe me when I was in school or at university, you would hear things like 'She's always winning', 'She's a go-getter', 'She takes no nonsense from anyone and knows exactly what she wants and where she's going in life'. So why was it that every time I was alone, that unsettling feeling of unfulfillment would creep back in? Don't get me wrong, I was still a happy, typical teenager, but I just always seemed to feel like something was missing – and I was completely right.

Many of us don't see that there's more to life than the particular stage we are at or what we are currently doing. We seem to get trapped in 'Well, I seem to be doing OK at life, so I guess I will just stick with that'. After all, we are creatures of habit.

Although there are many things I have learnt and improved on over the years, I was able to pinpoint one of my biggest issues: I was unable to enjoy the present moment. I was unforgiving of certain people that had hurt me in the past, therefore my motivation to do well wasn't coming from within; it was coming from a place of anger. I was tied to and stressing about things in the past that I couldn't change and where I had felt wronged. I was also angry at myself for allowing myself to go through certain situations that could have been avoided, or that shouldn't have lasted as long as they did, because I didn't have the courage or love myself enough to walk away.

I seemed to always be living in the future, not embracing the present, stressing about the past which I could not change, and like most others trying to fill this strange feeling of absentness and unfulfillment. Many of us think that we can fill this gap with clothes, jobs, relationships, friends, several courses, or degrees. In fact, these are the things I believe I personally used to mask my true feelings, things we believe we derive pleasure from, but only provided me with short-term fulfilment. Are you guilty of this?

I'd always come up with all these amazing ideas of what was going to make me happy, but really there was no destination because I didn't know what my happy looked like. It was like driving a car whilst the GPS is constantly re-calculating the route because it has no signal, so it can't figure out where it is going. Or firing a gun with no target. Eventually, you realize you need a target to focus on. You cannot be 'happy' until you know what happiness looks like to you, and even when you get there, it requires constant effort to maintain.

In April 2017, after a five-hour operation, I woke up a new person. It was like I had gone to sleep as one person, and my body decided it was someone else five hours later. My mindset was in a completely different headspace, and it was as if everything had suddenly just occurred to me. Although I had never looked like I was struggling, I felt at a disadvantage because I was in a job I no longer loved, I didn't know what I wanted to do, I had no set goals, and I felt that I was always doing so much for other people and not enough for myself. Suddenly, I felt like I had wasted so much time and the combination of all these things affected many aspects of my life. I was trapped in a subconscious cycle of doing what I always did, so I got the same results, which is why I always encountered the same types of feelings and problems.

When I started altering my habits, I noticed that my life started to change – and I have genuinely been a much happier and more content person ever since. It wasn't new things I did, but it was definitely things

I wish I had learnt at a younger age. Yes, we are only young once and we should enjoy our youth, but it will put you at a much better advantage if you invest in yourself and your future, because no-one is young forever.

I have always known that I wanted to inspire young people, but before I could do that, I needed to become the person I am today. I have been a hypocrite and I have been judgemental. My heart has been broken and has felt deep unfulfillment. I have made unrealistic comparisons, and believe me when I say I am far from being an angel, but It took years of work to become the person I have today. I want to share with you the lessons that have helped me become a better person, in the hope that anyone reading this can make positive, long lasting changes earlier than I did. And for anyone older reading this, I hope that this book inspires you to make a change in your life, too.

Once I made these changes and applied them to everyday life, there were noticeable differences in my personal and professional life. Suddenly everything started to make sense, things just began to click, I was able to truly be happy, and I had a sense of contentment and fulfilment.

It's not an easy journey, though. And you have to continuously apply the principles to your day-to-day life, never become complacent, and accept that you will still be learning every single day. You will have good days and bad days, and believe me I still do, but remember that happiness and fulfilment is not a destination but something you must work at constantly.

So, in order to help others avoid the quarter-life crises, I decided to write this book to give simple tools that will help improve your future self, because although people say 30s is the new 20s... it's not. Psychologist Meg Jay states that 80% of life's defining moments will have happened by your mid-30s. Personality and habit changes are harder after 30, and the first 10 years of your career often decides how much money you earn. So why wait to start life later when you can give yourself a head start by claiming your 20s.

# CHAPTER 1

# You Are Your Number One Priority

Loving yourself is an interesting concept that seems to be thrown around in society today. I find it annoying how we are always told to love ourselves but are never really given the tools or techniques on how to do so. What I have learnt is that physical beauty is not everything. Have you ever met someone who is beautiful but has a terrible personality? How quickly does their beauty diminish in your eyes? Even the opposite: how many times have you met someone that you did not find physically attractive, but their personality was amazing, and somehow their beauty seems to grow on you? It has happened to me multiple times. Both my family and friends say that I have dated quite a few 'ugly' people in my time, but this is because beauty is only skin-deep. And it is the same with loving yourself; it has to be based on more than what you look like, even though everything in today's society is telling you otherwise.

Don't get me wrong, your physical appearance is important, and you should take care yourself and how you look on a daily basis. But these standards should come from within, and should not be based on external factors such as magazines or people on social media that probably don't even look like that themselves. There is a significant difference between loving yourself and loving the way you look.

One of the main issues I've found when it comes to loving yourself is that we are not really taught how to do this in our adult years. As a child, you never really needed to learn to love yourself; most of us got a lot of love from our parents, family, and friends. We were constantly told that we were loved, or we were beautiful, but as you get older this slows down or stops, and at this point you have never really thought much about inward validation. Learning how to make the shift from outward validation to inward validation is difficult, especially when some of us don't even realise we are seeking outward validation.

Another issue is the rise in social media, which has us constantly comparing ourselves to the lives of others when we cannot prove that what they are posting is even real. Furthermore, we now live in a society where everything is buyable, and we can shop for everything. You want a new nose, new boobs, bigger lips, smaller hips; it's all shoppable, it literally takes a Google search or an Instagram hashtag, and you'll find what you are looking for.

What many people don't realise is that this will not change the way you see yourself; this only changes your physical appearance, and it's the wrong attitude to have. What you really must change is your relationship with yourself and work from the inside out; that is how you will begin to see the true beauty in yourself. This brings me to a conversation I was having with a friend of mine that I will never forget. He said, 'Women that have had multiple surgeries done to improve their looks always intrigue me. I wonder if they know or believe it shows a level of shallowness, but more importantly it reflects on their outlook on life and shows an attitude of a quick fix approach.' We continued this conversation for hours, and this reinforced my thoughts on how people are constantly changing things about themselves that they don't like – especially physically – yet don't challenge themselves to change internally. But I get it. Working on the mind is much tougher than working on the outside. Change on the inside takes time, effort, and consistency, which helps you to build resilience in life, and that is what you need. You don't have to be religious to understand this, but even the Bible says: 'Your beauty should not come from outward adornment, such as braided hair and the wearing of gold jewellery and fine clothes. Instead, it should be that of your inner self, the unfading beauty of a gentle and quiet spirit, which is of great worth.' As I said earlier, personality and strength are contagious, and beauty shines from within. When you feel good within, it reflects outwardly.

Don't misunderstand what I'm saying. I'm not completely against surgery, and if you believe that it makes you happy, do what you need to do! What I am against is the quick fix mindset because we all wake up every morning and decide to either love ourselves or pick ourselves apart. Isn't it interesting how you wouldn't go into school, university or work and pick apart your colleague or friends, saying exactly what you thought about their physical appearance or anything you disliked about them personally, especially if it was negative? But you're ok with doing it to yourself on a regular basis. Why? This is exactly what you need to learn not to do to yourself. You can't control if a thought comes into your mind, but you can change your thinking pattern and have a more positive outlook on yourself and life. It takes a conscious effort to love yourself the way you are, including all your flaws. After all, there is not one person in this world that was born perfect.

There are multiple ways to make yourself feel good and, let's be honest, a lot of the time we neglect these simple facts which is why we don't feel good. You don't have to look like anybody else to think that you're beautiful; you just have to accept yourself and understand that not everyone will think you are beautiful. I certainly don't think everyone is beautiful and neither do you, but you must understand that 'everything has beauty, but not everyone sees it'[1]. Once you understand that, you start to see things differently. Once you comprehend and appreciate that there is no other person like you in this world, that

---

[1] Confucius

alone makes you beautiful. Learn to be less critical of yourself. When you criticise yourself, you call more attention to the things you don't like, and these things manifest. Remember: 'People of all kinds can be beautiful – from the thin, plus-sized, short, very tall, ebony to porcelain-skinned; the quirky, clumsy, shy, outgoing and all in between. It's not easy, though, because many people still put beauty into a confining, narrow box... Think outside of the box... Pledge that you will look in the mirror and find the unique beauty in you.'[2]

Overall, there are multiple ways in which you can learn to love yourself. Firstly, you can do this by becoming more confident, and there are multiple facets that build this up and help you become more grounded in self-love. These include maintaining healthy boundaries and learning to say no, quitting the negative self-talk, fuelling your body and mind, and taking care of your physical appearance.

## Confidence and validation

People often think that confidence is a personality trait. While sometimes it is engrained within us and comes more naturally to some than others, confidence is a skill that we can build – and that is what you need to focus on. Learn to love not just your physical

---

[2] Tyra Banks – former supermodel, television personality, talk show host, actress, and author

features, but all your flaws and imperfections. Learn to love the things about you that are not physically attractive as well as the things that are physically attractive. Just to get started with this, have a list of things that you love about yourself so you can constantly call on it when you need to.

Complete this short activity to help you get started.

What are 15 things that you love about yourself; half must be non-physical

1. _____

2. _____

3. _____

4. _____

5. _____

6. _____

7. _____

8. _____

9. _____

10. _____

11. _____

12._____

13._____

14._____

15._____

Now read through this list daily to remind yourself. Feel free to write more than 15, especially the ones that don't just reflect your physical beauty. This will allow you to be more accepting of yourself as well as giving you a daily reminder of the good things about yourself that you don't consciously think of day-to-day.

Top tip – You could even put it on a Post-It note and stick it on the back of your front door, so you see it before you leave the house every morning. Or in your home office, now that so many of us have all been working from home.

## Learn to big yourself up

No-one is going to remind you daily about all the positive things about you, so you need to learn to remind yourself. Most people that meet me describe me as mad or crazy, and you know what? I love it. I do not want to be boxed; I want to absolutely and unapologetically be me all the time. When people ask me to describe myself and I say 'I'm 12 out of 10', you should see the look on their faces (priceless!). They look completely puzzled; in their heads they are thinking, *Why does this girl think she is above average, and secondly, how come she is crazy enough to say it?*

The answer is simple: I'm at the point in my life where I've accepted my flaws, so it's difficult for people to use them against me. Secondly, I understand that there is more to me than physical beauty. What amazes me is that people often ask, 'Why do you say 12 out of 10?' and I say because I'm disciplined, I work on myself daily, I'm positive, I work on my character and seek to improve daily, and I take care of myself because I understand that without health we have nothing – and you can see their facial expressions slowly changing.

The simple truth is many people don't take the time to focus on the positive aspects of themselves. They're too engrossed in all negative aspects about themselves or their lives, which most of the time can be changed with a simple choice or daily habit. But more importantly, the more you say positive things about yourself, the more it manifests in you and in your life, and the more you start to believe it.

What we tend to do is box ourselves because that's what society tells us or makes us do. It's unusual to think highly of yourself, as you're classified as arrogant, but people are ok for you to lessen yourself or are happy for you to pretend or feel smaller than you are, because that is what is familiar to them. People are afraid to shine because it's uncommon. But it's not about making yourself lesser to fit in; it's about growing and shining so that your aura unshackles others. It's about always being bigger and better than you were yesterday, and you will see what a blessing you become to the people around you. Marianne Williamson says, 'Our deepest fear is not that we are inadequate. Our deepest fear is that we are powerful beyond measure. It is our light, not our darkness, that most frightens us. Your playing small does not serve the world. There is nothing enlightened about shrinking so that other people won't feel insecure around you. We are all meant to shine as children do. It's not just in some of us; it is in everyone. And as we let our own lights shine, we unconsciously give other people permission to do the same. As we are liberated from our own fear, our presence automatically liberates others.'[3]

## Fitness

When I first started working out, it seemed like such a chore, and I initially got into fitness for all the wrong reasons. The quick backstory to this is that my mum used to call me chubby at almost every family occasion (very embarrassing, but don't worry, I've forgiven her now!), and I was dating a guy just after I left university

---

[3]   Marianne Williamson — *A Return to Love*

and he cheated on me with a girl who was slimmer at that time. As I was already insecure about my weight and I had attached the issue of cheating to that, I lost a lot of weight originally because the momentum came from anger and resentment. You better believe that it was not sustainable, though, because I was not doing it for me; I was doing it for someone and something else.

Although I always played sport, I actually hated going to the gym and I wouldn't have called myself consistent, but it got to a point on my journey that I had started reading lots of books/articles and listening to podcasts, and I noticed that fitness was something that almost all successful people had recognised as vital and had credited with helping them develop a solid mindset and a better physical body. So I started doing some research on fitness and what the benefits were. There were clearly multiple benefits in theory, but I had to put it into practice. After one month I honestly believe that I started to see and feel a difference in my physical appearance as well as my relationship with myself. I realised that:

- The gym leaves you feeling good when you leave, as happy chemicals are released.
- It helps boost your self-esteem and confidence, which improves your relationship with yourself.
- When you're eating well and working out regularly, you have a sense of control which

increases your confidence (as humans, we like to feel in control).

- Seeing your body change alters your attitude towards yourself.
- When you complete/attempt more demanding physical tasks, your self-confidence will rise.
- Every time you go to the gym you feel a sense of accomplishment.
- Regularly attending the gym vastly improves your mood and immensely boosts your energy.

I didn't really know where to start and I had no clue what I was doing, so I found a Personal Trainer to create a plan for me, and I followed his weekly plan and logged everything I ate on a food tracking app. I watched YouTube videos of every exercise before I went to the gym, and I asked PTs in the gym for help when needed. All this allowed me to better my organisational skills, boost my confidence, build resilience, and learn discipline.

Obviously, you can easily go and get your body altered (cosmetically changed) these days, but there are many risks and more importantly it does not prepare you mentally (discipline, focus, resilience) so you may continue to make the same mistakes because you have the same mindset and the same habits. I'm sure you have seen the quote 'evolve or repeat'; cheating the system/yourself means you repeat the same mistakes because you haven't repaired the direct issue. Facing the issue head-on means you're forced to confront it directly, which pushes you in the direction to evolve due to a shift in mindset. At first, working out will seem like a chore, then you learn its power. And when you do it for yourself, you start to see how things in your life align and how one aspect can overlap into another.

Develop a workout routine that works for you, and remember you don't need to go seven times a week. You don't even need to go to the gym; you just need to find an activity you enjoy and that is suitable for you. My current routine is gym three times a week, and some sort of sporting activity once a week. I'd advise you to try out new activities with friends to see if there is anything you like. Don't forget, you are going to have off days, and some sessions will not be as successful as others or you might be too sore to work out. But at the back of your mind always remember that when you work out, you look good, and when you look good, you feel good.

Exercise definitely does wonders for the mind, and it's argued to be one of the most underused tools for depression. Once you get an adequate exercise routine in place, you're setting yourself up for what's to come with a strong body and mind.

It's important not to become to obsessed, though, and remember that off days are normal. You are not always going to feel up to it, but you have to love yourself throughout the journey. If you start at 90KG, love yourself until you hit the goal of 80KG.

Get yourself a partner that can hold you accountable. And if you can, work out together, because motivation is just a starting point and fizzles out after a while. This is where having a strong mind and discipline comes in; it's about the habits we create and the standard we hold ourselves to. To wrap this up, confidence comes from loving who you are and being confident in how you feel about yourself. Eating well and working out helps you start looking at yourself from a different perspective.

Depending on my mood for the week and what life throws at me, I tend to try and do a minimum of three workout sessions, especially if I'm not doing my weekly sport. I plan out my week on a Sunday, and I use my work schedule to help me determine what activities I will be able to do for the upcoming week. I tend to do one-hour sessions, but if I'm pressed for time, I might do a 30 min HIIT workout.

A busy week for me might look like this:

| Monday | Tuesday | Wednesday | Thursday | Friday | Saturday | Sunday |
|--------|---------|-----------|----------|--------|----------|--------|
|        | HIIT    |           | HIIT     |        |          | Body Pump |

## A less busy week looks like:

| Monday | Tuesday | Wednesday | Thursday | Friday | Saturday | Sunday |
|--------|---------|-----------|----------|--------|----------|--------|
| Weight Training | HIIT | | Weight Training | | | Boxing |

Or

| Monday | Tuesday | Wednesday | Thursday | Friday | Saturday | Sunday |
|--------|---------|-----------|----------|--------|----------|--------|
| | HIIT | Strongman | Weight Training | | | Boxing |

Here is a list of activities. Circle the ones that you think you would like, and check if your local gym offers them. Alternatively, if you can get yourself a PT, get a plan from them or sign up to an online coaching programme (make sure you tell them how busy you are, so that they don't give you an unrealistic plan).

## Activities

| HIIT | Boxing | Full Body |
|------|--------|-----------|
| Aerobics | Kickboxing | Lean Legs and Abs |
| Water Aerobics | Body Pump | Leg Day |
| Swimming | Yoga | Chest |
| Strongman | Combat | Push Day |
| Strength and Conditioning | CrossFit | Pull Day |

## Maintain boundaries and learn to say 'NO'

Not knowing how to say the word 'no' is a destructive habit – that is the easiest way to put it.

We simply do not have enough time nor energy to do everything we want to do, especially if it is for other people. So, when you say 'yes' to everything, it's obvious that you can't differentiate between what is a distraction and what is an opportunity.

Once you say 'yes' to one opportunity, you are saying 'no' to another, and that could potentially be limiting you. It's like going for two job interviews and being offered both jobs; once you say 'yes' to one employer, you miss out on the potential opportunities provided by the second employer.

So, what's the big deal in not knowing how to say 'no'?

- Your priorities become subsequent to other people's priorities.

- Your time is not valued by friends and family.

- You spend more time doing things for others rather than for yourself or loved ones.

- You do not have time for R and R (Rest and Relaxation).

- You are more stressed and unfulfilled because you aren't doing things for the right reasons.

- You won't be able to say 'yes' to things that are important to you.

- It shows you are not making decisions based on your goal alignment or what's important to you.

- People do not respect your time.

When you learn to put yourself first, you set boundaries. People then start to take you more seriously, as well as valuing and respecting your time, because they know you will support them when you can. As humans, if something is always readily available, we value it less than we should; I'm not saying that's right, but after all we are only human. If you were told you had one more year to live, I guarantee you would live it differently to how you live it now.

When setting boundaries and learning to say 'no', you need to have a clear focus of what's important to you. You should set goals and milestones you want to achieve, and understand that you do not live to please people. Many of us say 'yes' so that people accept us, but remember they are probably using you for their own needs and that is why it's important that you honour yourself.

How do you know when you need to say 'no'?

How do you set boundaries?

You need to spend some time alone to understand what truly matters to you and what you need to do to optimise your life and achieve your full potential. Setting goals is significant as it helps you align activities with what you want to do, guiding you when you want/need to say 'no'. Learning to say 'no' gives you more energy to optimise life. For example, I have a close group of friends and I rarely stray from that friendship circle. Although I am sociable and very outgoing, I know who I want to spend time with and who I don't. So, I don't feel bad for saying 'no' to going to parties for a friend of a friend, as I am not obliged and I have other things that I could potentially be doing.

Spending time alone enables you to build mental strength, as you are alone with your thoughts –both negative and positive. Spending alone time also builds strength in yourself as you become less reliant on others and depend more on the connection with your inner self. What I don't understand is why we say 'yes' to things that we don't want to do or things that don't align with our goals. We need to understand that it's ok if we disappoint people sometimes, and if your friends are not fine with you saying 'no' sometimes, maybe you should consider getting new friends. You might never be enough for some people. Some may think you are selfish, but it is ok to be selfish sometimes, and you must know when to be selfless. When it comes to ourselves, we often need a period of selfishness which can be seen as a discovery period or a period of self-love.

Having a reputation for being a 'yes' man or woman doesn't necessarily mean it's positive; you can still say 'no' and be loving and caring. Furthermore, it's important to know your limits and to have boundaries, because you can't focus on several things at once and make them all successful (jack of all trades, master of none). So focus on what you want and learn to say 'no', so that you have more energy for life and the things you want to concentrate on.

When you have a clear focus and understand that you must honour yourself, saying 'no' becomes easier because you have a good insight of what's important to you. It's an art that must be developed, though, so start by saying 'no' to the small things and don't feel the need to explain yourself. Give yourself time to decide before giving an answer (consider if it's really something that you want to do).

## THE LESSONS

- ❑ There are no quick fixes in life.

- ❑ You are respected when you have boundaries and you learn to say 'no'.

- ❑ Spend time alone so that you learn to control your thoughts, or your thoughts will control you.

- ❑ If you don't evolve, you repeat past mistakes.

- ❑ Look after your body; when you have a strong body, you have a strong mind.

❏ Eat to nourish your body and you will automatically feel better.

❏ Saying 'no' increases your focus on what's important to you.

❏ Be kind to yourself – after all, you are all you have.

## MORAL OF THE STORY

Understand your worth, and never settle. Build yourself up as a person, because character is more valuable than appearance and the best outfit you can own is self-confidence. Do things that make you confident, even if it defies the social norm – normality is overrated anyway. When you love yourself truly and deeply, everything else falls into place.

# CHAPTER 2

# Goal-setting

Many people have a vision of what their life should look like in the future or what it should look like now, but what people don't understand is the difference between a plan, a goal, and a vision. It sounds like common sense (which is not actually common), but I don't think I knew how to set goals properly until I was in my early 20s. Although I am happy with what I have achieved so far, I believe I could have achieved much more if I'd known when I was younger how to accurately set goals that aligned with my visions. It is a skill I continue to use now and something we must work on regularly, because as we evolve, so do our visions. Therefore, goals and plans may need to be altered to suit both your short-term and long-term vision.

Firstly, let's talk about the difference between them all. You can have multiple visions, as they may change due to time or growth. Goals are created to help you achieve your visions. Some people will argue that they are short-term bursts of motivation whereas plans are in place to help you achieve your goals. Motivation might get you started, but as it's finite, you soon run out of motivation.

Goals and plans require discipline. Visions are long-term and do not require action, but goals are short-term and require constant action. When you complete a task/activity, you build momentum to move on to the next activity. Plans, on the other hand, help you break down what you need to do to achieve your goals. Plans give you clarity on the actions that need to be done.

My formula goes like this:

## Vision = Goals + Plans

| Vision | Goal | Plan |
|---|---|---|
| Maintain a healthy and balanced lifestyle | Lose 5kg by 4th September, 2020 | Eat in a calorie deficit.<br>• Track food<br>• Meal prep at the start of the week<br>• Have a food journal to ensure you don't binge-eat |
| | | Exercise regularly<br>• Have an accountability partner<br>• Go to the gym 3 times a week<br>• Go for a run once a week |
| | | Improve habits<br>• Take vitamins daily<br>• Make sure I sleep at<br>• least 7 hours a night |
| Have a property portfolio and manage properties in the future for additional income | Buy my first property at 25 years old, before my birthday on June 5, 2017 | Save at least £900 monthly<br>• £600 of my monthly salary to add to my savings towards my flat deposit<br>• Tutor 3 times a week for additional income |

Interestingly enough, a lot of us don't have visions or goals and this is damaging to our being, because when we are not progressing, we often feel trapped. I know I definitely did.

When we are not becoming, creating, or doing something that aligns us with a sense of happiness, purpose, or achievement, we feel unfulfilled. Yet many of us don't have an aim of where we are going in life. This doesn't mean you need to have it all figured out, but there should be a vision in place for certain aspects of your life to help you set goals to achieve that. Furthermore, if you don't have visions, goals, and plans, how will you know when you have arrived at your destination? You're not living life; life is living you.

Most people don't achieve their visions or goals because they spend time planning but don't back it up with action. I find more people talk about how much they are doing or going to do but have a lot less to show for it. These days, everybody is busy, but the real question is: are you productive?

Visions and goals give you something to aim for, and little daily/weekly victories and milestones are much better than being stagnant. Most people don't understand the importance of having visions and goals, but goals give you a benchmark to reach and a way to measure your progress. You wouldn't get into a car with no destination, so why people do this with their lives makes no sense whatsoever.

When you are thinking of a vision, you should have multiple aspects of your life in mind so that you know what you need to consider – for example, education, career, family, attitude, physical health. You may also have other things you want to take into consideration (charity or public service). We are all different so we will have different aims, and understand when you do this that you are doing it for you! Not everyone will support your journey, and many people will even go as far as telling you that you can't do this, but just let their words go in one ear and out the other.

Life is much more interesting when you take risks, live your life for you, and remember that all you have is now. If you fail or miss a goal, get up, shake it off, and keep it moving. There is no-one on this earth that has not failed at something, and actually one of the biggest failures of all time is not living life for yourself (be your first priority).

If I had known the power of goal-setting earlier in my life, I wonder where I would be now. It's paramount that you understand goal-setting is one of the most powerful ways to exploit your full potential and keeps you on the right path to success.

## Goals keep you locked in

When you have an aim, you know exactly where you are headed. When you catch a flight, there is a destination at the end; when you get in a car, there is a destination at the end; when you go to work, you know where you are headed. The point is that if you know where you're going, you're less likely to get lost. Although sometimes goals seem far off, we are always still aware of them. And even if we try to push them to the back of our minds, we still recognise when we are straying from them. Reviewing your goals regularly helps to keep them at the forefront of your mind; they keep us locked in. When they are at the forefront of our mind, they help us to recognise/exploit opportunities and to live our lives to the fullest.

As goals are measurable, they tend to propel us forward, because we can see when we are moving in the right direction and when we are backtracking. To achieve a goal, you must take small steps. It's the small steps that work together to help us achieve the big things.

The best tip I've learnt to achieving long-term goals is to live in the moment and put all the action into the day. In simple English, have your monthly and yearly plans in place, but the most significant key to success is executing your day-to-day plan. When you complete your daily to-do, you are one step closer to achieving your weekly, monthly, and yearly goals. This keeps you more encouraged and fulfilled.

When we picture the goal as a whole, we often see it as a bigger obstacle than it actually is. As a result, we can become easily discouraged thinking about how we are going to get there, leaving us feeling more discouraged and unmotivated. So, if you want to be happy and feel fulfilled, create daily plans and keep moving forward. It's about putting your energy into now rather than thinking about later; sometimes later never comes (now is all).

## Goals makes you accountable

Accountability is significant and is the link between the actions you are doing now and the goals you want to achieve later. As human beings – myself included – we like to be defensive and come up with excuses as to why we can't or didn't do something, but this is extremely harmful to progress and does not work in our favour. Personally, I am still working on the defensiveness, but I might have the excuses one slightly more figured out (we are all a work in progress). Here is a minor example that felt so significant to me that it made me add this accountability section.

I was recently umpiring a netball match for a team that I coach. Now, from the side-lines it is easier to see the faults of the players, which I was noting down so that we could review them in training. Although I could see how much the girls wanted to win, they kept on making silly mistakes, which cost them the game and they ended up losing by three points. On the coach home, I was sitting quietly and all I could hear was the girls coming up with lots of excuses as to why they lost the game, blaming the other umpire, and picking up on all the other team's faults.

As they continued, I remembered a podcast I had listened to; I believe it was Gary V speaking, and he said, 'Excuses are for losers.'[4] I turned around and gave them a little pep talk and said, 'Girls, you didn't lose because the other umpire was biased. You lost because you made silly mistakes, and that cost you the game. Sitting on the coach feeling sorry for yourself, and coming up with why you didn't win, does nothing for you. Actually, accepting that you guys made multiple errors and that's why you lost is better, because it teaches you what *not* to do next time. If you want to be league champions, you must behave like league champions.

Yes, losing isn't the best feeling, but what's even worse is being a sore loser! Take responsibility for what happened on court and reflect on the game tonight. In training, I will ask you all what mistakes were made, and we will work on them as a team to come back better for the last game of the season.'

The girls were doing what we all do regularly – blaming others, or finding reasons why we can't do what we want, or why we didn't achieve something, when really there is nobody to blame but ourselves. You are accountable for you, and sometimes you need to be hard on yourself and tell yourself the truth – the reason you didn't do it is because you were lazy, or you

---

[4]   James Houran, Ph.D., Dallas | Keith Kefgen, New York

weren't willing to give up your free time, or you just didn't have your priorities straight. Even if you strongly believe it's someone else's fault, find another way, because in the grand scheme of things no-one cares what your excuse was, is, or will be. Somebody in the same situation did it before; they found a way. And somebody else will still do it after.

I always knew I wanted to write a book to inspire/help people, but it took me three years to get it started, re-written, and edited. Why? Because I was lazy. When I stopped making excuses and started to complete my daily actions for the book, I started getting things done. My level of productivity increased, and in turn, I started feeling better about myself. The same will work for you.

Goals keep us accountable because they give us targets to aim for, which means we get to exploit our full potential and live life in a meaningful way.

Having goals helps us set out our plans, and nothing feels better than achieving the things you wanted to do, which takes you closer to your goal. Life will throw obstacles at you, but you have to learn to re-evaluate the plan and re-prioritise your list. You don't quit when things get hard; you have a goal to meet! You become more flexible, and you know when you go off-track that you are responsible to work it out, as it is your goal and no-one else's. They don't care about your goals, visions, or dreams, they are too busy working towards their own. So blaming other people when you are off-track is completely pointless. Remember, nothing will change unless *you* change, and the right time to accomplish any goal or dream is now, because there is no right time but right now.

## Sense of direction and purpose

Many people understand the purpose of having goals, yet it is bizarre that so few people set them. Goals are significant as they give you a target, and are therefore one of the most effective ways to achieve success and live a meaningful life. Goals give you a sense of direction, as you are working towards what you believe you truly want, and working daily on what you want can significantly transform your mental wellbeing and your life overall. This is because you aren't just accepting life; you're working for it day by day, and you're making it work for you.

The reason why we get a sense of direction from visions and goals is because they push us outside of our comfort zone and make us think about what we truly want, as opposed to just excepting what is. Who really wants to be going through life aimlessly? Leaving your life to chance means you end up going with the flow, doing what everyone else is doing, or making impulsive decisions which will eventually have you going back and forth in life or repeating unwanted patterns.

Goals give you clarity and help you to focus on what is important. Having goals in place and revisiting them regularly helps to keep you aware of what you need to do. It gives you clear direction on what you need to focus on – for example, spending less money, completing a workout, going out less, saying 'no' to family and friends, or simply waking up earlier to write a page of your book. The power of saying 'no' is relevant here because if something is not taking you towards your goal (unless it's fulfilling your needs in other ways), you need to question yourself on whether you should be doing it. That might even mean saying 'no' to yourself; sometimes we are the toxic person holding ourselves back.

Having clarity makes you focus on what truly matters and helps to avoid wasting time on pointless activities. The problem we have is that many people think we have lots of time, but the truth is that although time is infinite, it's not infinite for us. Time is possibly the most valuable currency in the world, as it cannot be stored or bought back. Once you spend that minute, hour, or day, you can never get that time back. You don't know what tomorrow will bring, so live fulfilled, working towards your goal today, feeling the pull from your sense of direction.

Goals help you to organise your life better, as certain aspects of your life become a priority, and they direct your focus in every area of life. Once you have a direction to head in, you will notice less short-term bursts of motivation but more consistency and energy towards your long-term vision.

Remember, though, dreams require sacrifice. So, every day when you get up, you have to ask yourself how much you really want something (remember the current status of your life is due to the standard you currently hold yourself to). And keep in mind that the most precious resource you can utilise is time; once time is wasted, you can never get it back, so you might as well give up a few things now for a better tomorrow. Make the sacrifice to read that book, cancel that party, or work towards your next career move, because although people say your 30s is the new 20s, that is honestly not true. The older you get, the quicker time passes you by, and it actually becomes harder to change and adapt. So start now, and be willing to make sacrifices for the life you want to live, a life you are proud of.

## THE LESSONS

- ❏ If you don't know where you're going, you're going nowhere.

- ❏ Life will live you if you don't live it.

- ❏ Power lies in the clarity of knowing what you want. If you don't know what you want, outside forces will dictate what you want.

❒ Failure is inevitable, so stop feeling sorry for yourself and keep moving forward.

❒ You can plan all day, but action is superior to planning, and nothing can be achieved without doing. So, do it – and do it now.

❒ Goals give you a direction which helps you determine your priorities.

## MORAL OF THE STORY

A large percentage of people live their lives, accepting life for what it is. As a result, their lives are curbed and restricted by comfort and simplicity. Confined by their own limitations. If you want to excel at life, knowing what you want is power. It is this power that will propel you forward to achieve success.

# CHAPTER 3

# Forgiveness

## Forgiveness and acceptance

When we hold onto things, events, or situations, they affect us mentally – and sometimes even physically – whether we want to admit that or not. Often, we subconsciously hold onto things that we think we have moved on from, and we allow them to fuel us for motivation or revenge. I have definitely been in that situation before, having done something just to spite someone, to prove a point, or just to get back at someone that hurt or angered me. I would go as far as admitting that I let the hurt or anger fuel me, and I used it as motivation.

Negative energy is negative energy, and our body and mind react and respond to this. I've noticed the more negative thoughts I have, the more negativity I see in situations, and the more negativity I call into my life. People don't often believe it, but have you ever noticed that when you're sad you seem to find sad people around you, and when you're happy, you find happy people are attracted to you?

Learning to forgive and accepting situations shows strength in your personal character. It does not mean you stand for or condone wrong-doing, it does not show your weaknesses, and it definitely does not mean you need to forget what hurt you. It's important to recognise the hurt and learn lessons from the situation, as learning to forgive actually increases your strength and frees you up to live in the moment. Being forgiving is liberating and actually keeps you free from carrying excess baggage from the past into your present and into the future. It frees us from negative thoughts and enables us to release negative energy. And when you release negative energy, it frees up more space for positivity in your life.

How do I know this? Because growing up I often felt hard done by in certain situations; these situations differed, but involved family, friends, and relationships, and at the time I didn't realise how I was affected as a person.

I honestly just believed I was a strong person, but now I realise the difference between being strong and having toxic traits. It's easy to misconstrue strong and salubrious characteristics with toxicity, and I'm definitely not the only person that has felt hard done by. Many of us have, but you can clearly distinguish between a forgiving and unforgiving person by their behaviour and their approach to life.

When you forgive someone or accept a situation that has happened, you grow! Sometimes it takes a lot of healing time to repair yourself, but this also teaches you more about what you're willing to accept and what you aren't (you learn your standards and boundaries). It also increases your resilience, which is a crucial life skill as it enables us to protect ourselves from stressful periods, toxic relationships, overwhelming experiences, and developing mental health issues, etc. What people tend to forget is that when you forgive, it is for your own benefit. In addition, sometimes it's important to evaluate yourself, take a moment to consider your own actions and what you have done to others, as we ourselves are not perfect. We have also hurt people in one way or another, therefore we need to think about the emotional damage we may have inflicted on someone. And although it's easier to dismiss when you have hurt someone, think about how long it may have taken them to recover or to move on from that. Look inward and reflect on a time when you needed someone to forgive you, think about how you felt when they forgave you, and think about how it felt if they didn't.

It's funny, when we stay angry or we harbour negative emotions towards someone or something, what you need to actually think is who the situation is affecting more: you or the other person. Realistically it is affecting you more, because you are the one reliving the negativity, which affects your mind, body, and life. And yes, the body can physically react to negativity.

It takes a lot of energy to remain angry/bitter, but at the end of the day life will happen to you and you must learn to grow through it and not stay in a negative state. Remember, life happens to everyone, which does not mean you push your feelings to the side; it means you work through it and let go. Everybody is dealing with a situation that isn't ideal, and we've all been hurt by someone, but when you do not accept or forgive, you're giving up your personal power. When you forgive or accept the situation, you are taking back your personal power and regaining control over your life; you build strength and learn to be more flexible should similar situations occur in the future. When you move on, it's not about forgetting what the other person did or what has happened, it's about moving on to the future without harbouring negativity. It's also about understanding that in every situation there's a lesson, and you have the choice to decide on your attitude, emotions, and feeling towards it.

It's imperative we learn to free ourselves from emotional baggage, as the more you relive or dwell on a situation/relationship, the deeper-rooted or more planted the issues become. You build strength and pliability when you free yourself, your heart, and your mind from emotional stress. It does not show weakness in you; in fact, it shows great strength, because anybody can be bitter and hold a grudge, but it takes great courage to forgive and move on.

The heart, thoughts, and mind are to be protected, and forgiving and accepting is one of the keys to this. There is a reason why the heart is protected by the ribcage and why the Bible says to guard your heart.

One significant life lesson I've learnt is to forgive quickly as it frees you from a heavy heart. You don't want the feeling of hate, hurt, or bitterness to grow, because it means you are nurturing it. You can't plant an apple tree and expect to see pears, so you can't possibly harbour or dwell in negativity and expect to see positive results. Strength comes from accepting, forgiving, and moving on, as life waits for no-one. Having the courage to forgive will only empower your future.

## THE LESSONS

❐ You can't stop life from happening to you; it happens to everyone.

❐ Bitterness poisons you from the inside out, so be mindful what you let/keep in.

❐ To forgive quickly builds strength and shows great courage.

❐ When you forgive, it does not mean you need to forget. Learn from it.

❐ In difficult situations, you build resilience.

❐ Learning to accept and forgive helps you to claim back personal power.

❐ You harm yourself more when you harbour negative emotions.

❐ Forgiving frees you from emotional baggage and enables you to feel empowered with hope for the future.

## MORAL OF THE STORY

Forgiveness does not come naturally, but it's one of the best gifts you can give yourself. To forgive does not show great weakness, but in fact shows great strength; it takes courage to push through measures that sometimes we don't expect. Do yourself a favour and free your heavy heart and stop reliving situations that almost tore you apart.

# CHAPTER 4

# Social Circle and Relationships

People love to downplay the influence their relationships with friends, family, and partners have on them and their lives. Everyone loves to say, 'I am my own person and what my friends do is their problem.' Whilst you are 100% your own person, the people around you still play a significant role in your life, especially as you navigate through your 20s.

Growing up, I heard so many sayings like 'birds of the same feather flock together' and 'tell me who your friends are and I'll tell you who you are'. Back then, I used to completely disagree, but now I understand why those sayings are constantly repeated, because you really are as good as the company you keep. Have you ever noticed at school or work how you naturally gravitate towards people that are the most like you? This could be dependent on race, socio-economic background, behaviour, or personality traits. Sometimes, even if you aren't the one in your friendship group doing negative things, you're just guilty by association. You need to select friends that reflect the lifestyle you want, or friends that have achieved or are in alignment with your own goals, aspirations, and personal characteristics.

It took so long for me to realise this, and I wish that someone had explained in more detail the importance of friendships and relationships earlier, as opposed to just word vomiting irrelevant quotes. Who understands the impact of their social circles at 15 or 18 years old? At that age, we are just learning how to figure ourselves out. An old Japanese proverb says, 'When the character of a man is not clear to you, look at his friends'[5]. So the type of people you have in your immediate circle speaks volumes about you and what you stand for. If you think back to Chapter One, which discusses loving yourself, you are careful about who you let in your space, especially if you have a lot you want to achieve and you have placed yourself as your number one priority.

It's vital that you surround yourself with the inspired, the hard-working, and the dedicated. Who you surround yourself with is who you essentially become. If your four closest friends are lazy and broke, eventually you will become the fifth lazy and broke friend. It is better to be alone building your empire and working on your unlimited potential than mixing with the wrong company.

Let go of negative people in your life – family or friends. Life is hard enough as it is, and you don't need anybody poisoning your space, mind, and life. We all have bad

---

[5]  Japanese Proverb

days and it's good to be supportive of people, but know the difference between supporting your family and friends and putting yourself out. I learnt this lesson very quickly after university. I had a friend who I thought I couldn't live without. We had known each other for over five years, and she had always been there in my time of need, and vice versa. But our relationship was not healthy at all. It's like we had obsessive compulsive disorder with one another; the relationship was so toxic it wasn't worth the negative effect it was having on my mental health. As I was growing as a person, I knew this friendship was not going to better me in any way, so I had to let that friendship go as a result of the growth I was experiencing in my personal life.

## You're only as good as the people you walk with

If you're rolling around with losers, you're either already a loser or you will become one. You can try to make excuses and justify why this is not the case, but remember that iron sharpens iron, and that is the God's honest truth. It's very difficult to develop as an individual when you're surrounded by people who aren't growing themselves. The people closest to you will determine whether you grow or not. It is possible to outgrow people, which means your friendship group needs to evolve, too. You want to change something in particular about your life, physical, or mental wellbeing? Then hang around with people that are already where you want to be, as that will force you to level up. When you see people around you that are doing amazing things, you begin to feel inspired, and you start to see things differently. You begin to feel encouraged and motivated, you start dreaming, and this can force you to level up and push you outside of your comfort zone. Life is competitive, and nobody wants to be the loser of the group. A minor example is when I was working as a teacher and living in London, and most of my colleagues in my department had a Masters degree. I was the youngest in my department and they all encouraged me to go and get my Masters. Before I left that place of work, I had achieved my MSc in Strategic Management.

In addition, a lot of my friends at this time were super into health and fitness; some loved CrossFit and the gym, others were runners, and some were PTs. Even though I was already into the gym, it forced me to level up my gym game and learn more about nutrition. But when I moved to Dubai for two years, I started to focus less on my body, gym, and nutritional goals, because the people that were surrounding me at that particular time cared less about these things and were more into partying, so naturally that's the behaviour I fell into (love you, girls, but it's true).

While we are growing in our 20s, our goals and views are constantly changing. But it's essential that you have a picture of what and who you aspire to be within the next couple of years, then surround yourself with people who will force you into being a better version of yourself. It is important that you surround yourself with the grateful, the inspired, the motivated, the passionate, and the open-minded; find friends that add value to your life and not constantly detract from it.

Having positive friends genuinely helps with your outlook on life. If you're surrounded by positive people, your life will drastically improve, as will your perspective and outlook on life, as well as your drive to do well. Naturally, my friends approach me for all types of reasons, but when they want to get serious advice, they ask me because they know I'm not going to pussyfoot around. I'll tell them the honest truth, and I would expect/get the same in return. Having friends that are supportive and honest helps to inject more meaning and fulfilment into our lives. When you have friends that are of value, it enables you to open up, have great conversation, and discuss your successes. Real friends clap for you and help put things into perspective. They smile at your successes, and you should do the same.

## Let go of toxic relationships.

Some of us have toxic relationships and we don't even know what toxic means: very unpleasant or unacceptable"[6], or poisonous.

Understanding that friends, partners, and families can

---

[6]  https://dictionary.cambridge.org/dictionary/english/toxic

all be toxic is crucial, and my advice on managing toxic people is to love them from a distance. The type of energy that you let into your space is so important that it is talked about consistently across the globe, whether it be in self-help books, talk shows, or podcasts.

The question often asked is: what are the signs of a toxic relationships? Sometimes it is very hard to recognise.

Here are some of the signs of being in a toxic relationship (friends, family, or partners):

- They never say sorry as they don't like to take responsibility for their actions.
- Unsupportive and undermining.
- Manipulative and negative.
- Self-obsessed.
- Never the optimist; always has a negative comeback to all your solutions.
- They bring out the worst in you.
- Jealousy or controlling behaviour.
- You feel the need to constantly walk on eggshells around this person.
- They take without giving.
- They like to play the victim.

As we know, you are who you associate yourself with. Therefore, if you are very close with an individual who exhibits toxic behaviour, it is just a matter of time before you start to exhibit toxic traits. Remember, bad character corrupts good nature. The only thing that will happen is you will become more toxic, bitter, and irritated. You will never be able to truly change a toxic person, so you might as well remove them from your life, because toxic behaviour is contagious.

Another reason to remove toxic people from your life is to simply avoid being pulled into a range of different issues/crises. These people make it seem like they need you, but often this will begin to pull you down because a lot of the time they are creating their own problems, and dwelling on these problems won't make things any better. You will also begin to see that when you give them a positive solution, they will only come back with a negative one. Remember, toxic people have a way of projecting their issues onto you, but this is just because most of the time they are unhappy with themselves, so attacking you or bringing you down may be their only way to feel better. But guess what? You don't have to let that happen.

Here are some stories for you!

## Story 1

A friend of mine was in a relationship, and when she and her partner first started dating everything was amazing. You know, the honeymoon period is always remarkable. After a while, though, she noticed some flaws in his character; he was always quite negative, very pessimistic, and found a problem to every solution she would give him (bear in mind, she is an optimist).

One day he lost his job and began to project his own personal issues onto her and everyone around him. He was constantly saying negative things to her and even stopped engaging with her sexually. Eventually it got so bad that the relationship gave her very bad anxiety, and she started having full blown panic attacks when they would argue. The relationship began to take from her rather than uplift her.

As friends, we tried to support her through the problems, but ultimately it gets boring listening to the same thing every day. In the end, the other girls in our friendship group just stopped engaging, and it got to a point where I was so bored of hearing the same thing every day that I just told her what I thought was best to do in the situation and left it to her to make the best decision for herself.

She eventually got tired of how this relationship was affecting her mental health, which was now having a physical impact (panic attacks) on her, and she left. She explained that she'd thought she could change him, but most importantly she'd learnt her own personal boundaries, and how the impact of a negative relationship/person can really affect all aspects of your life. She is now happily married to someone else.

## Story 2

Julie had a best friend who she thought was extremely supportive, but eventually time showed that her best friend was not her biggest supporter and was actually her biggest doubter. Julie was a go-getter and started doing things very young. For example, she was learning how to drive at 17, and her friend would always say, 'Don't you think it's too early to start? You don't need to worry about this now.' Any time she would be around certain friends that motivated her, Julie's best friend would always make comments like, 'They can do that, but you can't because of your background' and 'You don't have the money'. It got to a point that anything positive Julie was doing in her life, her best friend would find something negative to say. When Julie went on to do her Masters, her friend said, 'I don't see why you are doing this. I can't see how this would benefit you. This is wasting your time.' When Julie bought her first flat in London, her friend was making comments, saying, 'I could have done that, but I had other priorities' and wasn't celebratory of Julie. Eventually, Julie felt uncomfortable sharing her success with her best friend, and it got to a point where even when she did want to do certain things, she didn't because she wasn't sure how her friend would react. Finally, Julie realised she had to let this friend go, as she knew this friendship would only hinder her.

Sometimes you think your family and friends have your best interests at heart, but that is not always the case. Ever heard the saying 'They want to see you do good, but they don't want to see you do better than them'? This is most definitely true when you do not have the right people around you.

Although people may be rooting for you, sometimes they are secretly in competition with you, which can also mean that they are furtively hoping for you to fail. It may not always pose itself as outright competition, but sometimes it's subtle discouragement, like giving you 100 excuses as to why you can't start a business or why you can't achieve something.

When people are not as supportive as you expect, it's important to remember that this has nothing to do with you, because people are often projecting their own limitations onto you. You must know who is for you and who is not. But, regardless of the situation, do not take their negativity or discouragement to heart. Train your mind to be stronger than your emotions, keep the momentum going, and protect your space.

Every person that has seen success was once told they couldn't do it or that they wouldn't make it. But with constant action, clear goals, and the right people, their goals were achieved.

Having toxic people in your circle only reflects how you feel about yourself. Think back to Chapter One: if you love yourself, you will have strong boundaries in place and you treat yourself with respect and dignity; you will not allow people to treat you inadequately. Having a friend, family member, or partner, that treats you badly with your acceptance shows lack of self-respect and self-confidence.

## How can you remove toxic people from your life?

- Forgive, but don't forget.

  Remember, forgiveness is a gift to yourself. You don't want to hold onto anything that will make you bitter, but don't forget their behaviour so you can easily move on with your life.

- Set boundaries.

  Set clear boundaries and enforce them. Ensure you stick to these boundaries. It's possible people will try to manipulate you, but it's important you stand your ground.

- Cut them off completely or make a run for it.

  Sometimes the easiest way to make a clean break is to go cold turkey. I have found that this works for me, and the easiest way is to block, delete, and keep moving. This helps me maintain my own personal wellbeing.

- Don't expect them to change.

  As human beings, we will almost always put ourselves first. I'm not a mother yet so my view on this may change, but nevertheless the point still stands that we have our own best interests at heart. Therefore, a toxic person may not change, as they're too deep rooted and motivated by their own problems. It's easier to let them go than try to change them; and yes, sometimes it's ok to take the easy option.

– Accept the loss and be grateful for the lesson.

It can sometimes be very difficult to let go because it can leave a void, but understand that time heals everything, and sometimes it's better to put yourself first and accept the loss, because everyone you meet has taught you something – whether the lesson is positive or negative.

## THE LESSONS

❐ Take care of yourself first; you deserve it. You can't take care of someone else if you can't look after yourself ('you can't pour from an empty cup').

❐ Do not think you can change people. It's more than a full-time job changing yourself.

❐ Be mindful of friends and family that don't clap for your successes.

☐ If you are the most successful in your group, you need a new group, and vice versa. If you're uninspired by the people you surround yourself with, you guessed it... you need a new group.

☐ Life is too short to condone mediocre relationships of any sort.

☐ Never let anybody make you feel like you're second choice, and be willing to walk away from anything that threatens your peace.

☐ You're only as good as your five closest friends.

☐ Let go of toxic people. There is no point watering a dead plant – remember, the grass is greener where you water it.

## MORAL OF THE STORY

You can't water a dead plant and expect it to grow, so don't think you can change a toxic person. Let go of toxic people and don't be blindsided. Learn to foster positive relationships; the grass is greener where you water it. You are your actions, so be involved with people who are already where you want to be. It is the fastest way to evolve.

# CHAPTER 5

# Comparisons steal your joy

*'Comparison is the thief of all joy'* –
*Theodore Roosevelt*

*'A flower does not think of competing with the
flower next to it, it just blooms.'* – *Zen Shin*

Not comparing yourself to others is a lot easier said
than done, like most things in life. It is good to be
inspired by others and aspire to be like them, but there
is a difference between aspiring to be and comparing
to.

'Aspiring to be' has a positive connotation, but
'comparing to' does not; the term comparing is
normally associated with negativity and often focuses
on what you lack. When you compare yourself to
others it is the start of a losing battle, because where
does it end?

In life, we are supposed to learn from one another and
find inspiration to encourage each other on our own
individual journeys. But we forget that everybody's
journey will be different, because life has different
things in store for us; we all have different wants and
desires. You have to be able to trust the timing of your

own life and accept that your life will come in different stages or seasons; sometimes it will be summer, sometimes spring, or it might even be a rough winter/rainy season.

If you are constantly trying to be the best amongst people, where will you find joy in that? But more importantly, you are not going to be better than everyone all the time, nor should this be your aim. You should aim to be the best version of you.

When I worked in a school, I often met mothers and fathers at parents' evening who wanted to know if their child was the best in the class. And I'd hear them say to the child, 'If he or she can get a Level 7, why are you on a Level 5?', instead of celebrating their child's achievements. What they fail to understand is every person's ability is different. What may be seen on the surface is not always a true reflection of reality.

I personally believe the child would do much better if the parent said, 'Well done for getting a Level 5, I know you worked hard! Next time you have a test, let's work together to get you to a Level 7.' That would not only discourage comparison, but would help the child to build a better mindset about working for and on themselves. Instead, all this parent did was to create unnecessary envy, because now that child was going to focus on trying to get the same grade as another child, rather than focusing on themselves and where they could improve.

If anything has become apparent in the era of social media, it's the fact that we should not use other people's success or progress as a benchmark for ourselves. Not only is jealousy and envy ugly, but it hinders us from genuinely celebrating the success and accomplishments of others. Remember, life always comes in seasons. You cannot compare your Chapter 12 to another person's Chapter 22. Plus, everything is based on perception; you see what you want to see, therefore comparison can rob you of your joy, yet you may be comparing yourself to a perfect illusion that may not even exist. Looks can be deceiving.

Sometimes, we compare ourselves because we believe we have worked just as hard or even harder than someone else and we may feel overlooked. This happens because in some situations we play on an uneven playing field. Life every so often just isn't fair, and some people are born with more advantages than others. But there is no point beating yourself up over circumstances you can't control, so don't compare yourself as it does not do you any favours. Instead of putting yourself down or negatively comparing yourself to others, play your own game, not theirs. Everyone is dealt different cards in life.

## Story 1

A woman I know was dating a guy, and in the first six months everything was going extremely well (obviously the honeymoon stage). As things progressed, she started to get to know the person more and the perfect illusion put up in the beginning began to crumble bit by bit; she saw the person for who he really was. The guy had initially been by no means perfect, but little things started to happen in their relationship and the woman began to doubt him, becoming unsure whether she wanted to stay with him or not. After a few weeks apart, she decided that she wanted to break up as she didn't think he was the right man for her. During that time, she met another guy who seemed to have it all together and what the girl originally thought she wanted in a man; he was offering her the opposite of her ex. He was a businessman, relatively well travelled, a trained accountant, and was confident in himself. The two became friends and hit it off straight away, and the chemistry was undeniable – or so she thought, anyway. After a few months of talking and seeing each other, though, cracks also began to appear, and he started to show similar characteristics to her previous partner along with some traits that were worse. The point here is that sometimes you compare incorrectly.

There's no such thing as perfection. Illusions are real, and a lot of the time we only see what we want to see. We tend to see the positive aspects of other people's lives; therefore we have a misunderstanding of the behind-the-scenes background work that has permitted them to live the life they are living, or to be in the position that they currently are.

People tell you or show you exactly what they want you to see. For example, how many of us take 100 pictures before we post one on Instagram? I know I'm guilty. How many of us discuss our failures with family and friends as often as we discuss our successes? We hide away our failures and tend to present our best self, whether it be in real life or on social media. What's funny is that the failures allow for the most growth.

Don't get me wrong, we are all guilty of sometimes hiding our failures. For example:

- When I graduated from my Masters, I just posted the picture. I didn't post when I failed one assignment by one mark, and I had to redo it.
- My cousin wrote a book, and it has done amazingly well, but she never posted the numerous rejections she first received from publishers.
- People are going through separations yet are still posting images of a happy family.
- People present as body confident or post amazing aesthetic pictures, but have hidden eating disorders.

It's important to understand that what you hear and see can sometimes be deceiving. Don't get me wrong, social media can be a great source of inspiration, but it's important that you are able to see it as inspiration and not the whole truth, because it is pretty much created perfection which does not exist. We only see a small percentage of what somebody's life is actually like, but we know the full story behind our own lives.

## How to stop comparing yourself to others

- Water your own grass.

    The grass always looks greener on the other side, but believe me it's not. We know the ins and outs of our own situation and we tend to focus more on the negatives. As we are more critical of ourselves, we focus on what we don't have as opposed to what we do have. The trouble is, you don't know what somebody else doesn't have; you just know what they do, and you don't even know what they went through to get there. So, focus on your own garden, root out your weeds, water your grass, and feed your plants. When you look after your own grass, it grows.

- Limit your time with social media or do a social media detox.

    Although social media can be a great source of motivation, it has also created a society in which we constantly compare ourselves, which is dreadful for our mental health. Everybody is at a different stage in life, and sometimes we compare our Chapter 3 to someone else's Chapter 13, or we compare our winter season to someone else's summer. You don't know what people are going through offline, so it's important to remind yourself to be present in your own life and stay in your own lane. Remember, social media is an illusion; people post what they want you to see.

—   Understand that you are you biggest competitor.

The more we learn to be present in our own lives, the more we understand that in life everybody is meant to win, and we all have imperfections. So, compare yourself to who you were yesterday so that you become better not bitter. Ask yourself questions like how you could improve the quality of your life; or what positive habits you should work on; or what negative habits are holding you back.

Don't let society paint pictures of what you should be or have. Don't think to yourself, *I should be married at 24, I should have a house by 27, or have kids by 30.* What you should do is focus on your own life and work towards achievements you want instead of the 'I should'. Trust the timing of your life and run your own race.

'I should' makes us focus on what we lack, and the more you focus on what you lack, the more you call that into your life. So, stay in your own lane, as there will always be somebody smarter, richer, or more attractive than you, but guess what? That's life, and life is not fair.

— Be grateful.

It is easy to focus on what we lack or the less desirable aspects of our lives. It takes courage and motivation to maintain a positive mindset. Sadly, many of us wait until we have aged, or after a life-changing experience to appreciate the positive things in life. There is no time like the present, be grateful for what you have now; be thankful for all the things that you do have. There are things that you possess that other people only dream of.

## THE LESSONS

☐ When you focus on you, you become better not bitter.

☐ Everybody goes through different seasons, so work through your winter seasons.

☐ Don't compare your Chapter 3 to someone else's Chapter 13.

☐ Social media is an illusion; don't buy into it.

❐ Instead of focusing on what you lack, give thanks for what you currently have, and work towards what you want.

## MORAL OF THE STORY

Be content with where you are, and deal with the cards you are dealt. You can never win a race if you're constantly concentrating on the other contestants. Comparison causes misdirection and lack of focus, and if you want to win, you must be all-in. So do not try and keep up the same pace as someone who is running their own race.

# CHAPTER 6

# Finance

Dealing with or managing your finances is an important tool to be successful, and this doesn't necessarily mean you have to have money in abundance (even though I'm sure we would all love that). It is more the art of learning to deal with your finances.

Although many people could benefit from financial advice, many shy away from talking about it due to lack of knowledge or a feeling of embarrassment. But the younger you become more financially literate the better.

I've lived for 28 years and I have spent lots of money – some wisely, and a tremendous amount not so wisely, if I'm being completely honest. What I have learnt, or rather what life has taught me, is it's important to become financially literate earlier rather than later, and it's something I will teach any child of my own from a young age.

The steps in this section will not be things you haven't heard before; they're tools that we often need reminding of as we never stick to them, but it reaches a point where you know you really need to.

When you're young it is easier to become more financially literate because you have less financial responsibility. Obviously, this isn't the case for everyone, but generally speaking many young people don't have a family to look after, a mortgage to pay, or any excessive bills, yet we still find ourselves living pay check to pay check, with high credit card bills and no emergency fund. This is why basic understanding of finance is important as it makes us maximise our income no matter how much we earn.

The worst thing we can do when dealing with money is to say we don't earn enough and 'if I earned more, I would be able to do more'. That is the downfall of most people. The trick is to do the best you can with what you have. If you don't learn money management when you have less, you will find that you still waste money when you have or earn more. This is the constant cycle/trap that most people tend to get stuck in. We can't live for money; the key is to rule money and use it to the best of our ability, as opposed to letting money rule us.

Another issue that arises when dealing with finances is that it requires a lot of patience – something we don't have much of these days, due an entitled mindset and the instant gratification culture. Unfortunately, we seem to be trapped in this mindset of 'now', which makes us try to run the race as a sprint when really, it's a marathon. Money management requires consistency, patience, and time.

It's all about a shift in mindset, but the instant gratification style of life has our thoughts locked that we can do most things with the tip of our fingers. Fancy a burger? Just use an app. Can't be bothered to drive? Just use an app. Want to go on a date? Just swipe left and right. This is no fault of our own, but it's just the way the world is advancing due to technology.

## Stop relying on credit cards

We've all been there, let's be honest. It's one of those things that you can easily get sucked into, and you better believe I was a sucker when I received my first credit card. One day I was managing it well, then I blinked, and it was at £3000. At the time, that was more than my monthly salary. But, what was worse was I couldn't even tell you where that money had gone. It was probably spent on irrelevant, meaningless things such as food that ended up in the toilet, and clothes that I either wore once or twice. Some of the items I had never worn or used, and I ended up giving them to charity, but guess what? I still had to pay back that £3000 credit card bill. So, when I use my credit card now, I use it more carefully and with a lot more discipline. I would say I have semi-mastered the art of discipline whilst using my credit card, and I say semi-mastered because I'm obviously still a human being. However, I did stop using my credit card for three years until I felt confident enough to use it again.

Now I am more educated and understand how to use it better, I use it to build my credit, but I make sure I am not spending beyond my means and I ensure that I can always pay it back in full at the end of the month.

The point is that credit cards are a last-minute resource to use, not an everyday thing. Have a limit of how much you want to spend on the card monthly and make sure you don't go over it, otherwise you start paying interest, which means more money is lost. If you feel like you have no self-control but want to put in measures to ensure you pay it back each month, reduce your credit card amount. It is as simple as that.

Having good or great control over your finances will enable you to live a more stress-free life, and you'll be a lot happier for it.

## Have a side hustle

I started reading a book about side hustles years ago, and in the entire book I didn't feel like there was an idea that worked for me. I knew I was obviously good at being a teacher at the time, so I decided to start tutoring. I started teaching at 22, but I only started tutoring at 26. I could have just started when the idea first came to mind, but instead I waited for four years, which underlines the point that we underestimate ourselves and overlook the little things. When I started tutoring, the additional income was useful, and I thought, I'm definitely going to continue this and find something else I like to do. One day, whilst I was sleeping, another idea came into my head. I noticed that people always complimented me on my false eyelashes, so I thought: why not start with a small eyelash business as well, but doing both boxed lashes and individual eyelash extensions? Within one month, I had the boxed lashes ready, and within two months, I had completed my individual eyelash extension course and started doing individual eyelashes. That business still runs today, and it was actually funded from the money I received from my first side hustle (tutoring). All this additional money has a purpose, and I'm currently working on bringing in another side hustle which was inspired by my little cousin. Remember, when you listen, you can learn a lot – and you can learn from anyone.

## Live below your means

I would argue that this is the hardest things for most of us, especially as we are in the era of social media. These days everybody is trying to portray a particular lifestyle or trying to keep up with their friends, but that can potentially run you down both financially and mentally. Life is about staying in your own lane and running your own race. And once you find happiness from within yourself and you feel you don't need validation from external sources, you win!

When you understand yourself and have a better understanding of what's important, you learn to stay within your lane. We are only human, and we will still slip up, but the ability to live within or below your means is what separates the majority of people living that pay check to pay check life from the minority of people who aren't.

I'm not saying that it's an easy process, as it will involve a lot of research and, more importantly, a lot of patience and sacrifice. Ask yourself, in the era of instant gratification: what are you willing to give up? Despite all of today's challenges, there are still ways in which we can live within or below our means, so let's get to it.

The most obvious thing is knowing how much you earn. It sounds ridiculous, but if you know how much you make, then why are you overspending? You can't have a £5000-a-month lifestyle on a £3000-a-month salary.

The second step is to list all the bills, debts, and subscriptions you have. We waste a lot of money paying for unused subscriptions, interest and fees for minimum payments, unused gym memberships, etc. So, cancel anything you don't use, and don't sign up to things you don't need or won't make use of.

Step three is to understand all your bills and what dates these payments are coming out of your bank account. Again, this is another easy step yet so many of us get it wrong. Look at your list of bills and debts, then automate your payments so that they come out of your account two days after your pay goes in. Always ensure there is contingency in your account, so that your bills don't bounce.

This way, slowly but surely, everything is eventually paid off (have patience). Also, make sure you set up an automated payment for savings. You don't have to start big; start as small as you like, but ensure you always have something saved in an account that is not so easily accessible to you. That way you have money in case of an emergency, and undoubtedly that day will come.

When arranging your bills, you want to make sure that you are avoiding constantly being in overdraft. Once you understand how much you make, everything needs to be within that limit. You still need to ensure that you have enough left in your bank account to tie you over until the next month.

Again, as I touched on previously, learn to say 'no'. I mean, honestly, must you go to every party, dinner, baby shower, wedding, or holiday? Absolutely not. Yes, sometimes we want to treat ourselves, but how many times do we use this as an excuse? I have definitely been guilty of this. Honestly, I was always saying, 'it's been a long hard week, let me treat myself' and then I was getting to the end of the month, wondering where all my money had gone and, as usual, having nothing to show for it. Don't let this be you.

## Understand the difference between wants and needs

The average person has a lot of debt, let's be honest, whether that's student loans, credit card bills, car or mortgage repayments. Now I don't know about you, but becoming better with my finances was key for me because I had become tired of living that pay check to pay check life. Even now I am still working at it daily to become better. One big thing that helped me was understanding what I needed as opposed to what I wanted. A lot of the time we blur the two. Don't get me wrong, life is for living, so SOMETIMES you do have to get yourself some of those wants. But what I do now is I wait a few days to see if I really want that product or item, and if I'm still thinking about it then I go back and get it, or wait to see if I can find a discount code, or until the product has some money off. Some people might call that cheap, but I call it smart, as I try to stick to 20% payment of my income on wants and 30% to savings, while the rest goes on needs and investments.

## Savings and emergency funds

I learnt the importance of having an emergency fund the easy way; I just watched certain friends and family members, who didn't have any savings, suffer. They say a wise man learn from his mistakes, but a wiser man learns from the mistakes of others. Now, I know I shouldn't be smug about it, because they say experience is the best teacher, but sometimes it's a lot easier and saves us a lot of stress in the long term to learn from other people's experiences.

Whilst I'm still building my own emergency fund, I know I have to make certain sacrifices, but my monthly savings target is not one of them. I know I must hit it every month, and it means I have to work a full-time job and maintain two side hustles.

Having an emergency fund gives us some sense of security, because we don't know what the future holds. Again, set this up as an automated payment to an account you don't have easy access to. If you don't force the art of handling money, money will force your hand.

Tips

- Reflect on your finances monthly.
- Print off your bank statement and highlight everything you didn't really need (I hate this activity; it shows you how much money you waste).
- Have a finance plan.
- Always look for deals and discounts.
- Do not impulse shop.
- Cut up the credit card.
- Pay your debts on time.
- Find out about and take full advantage of employee benefits.

- Check your credit score regularly.
- Give back, even if it's just to one charity – if you can't give now, you will find it hard to give later, so learn the art of giving, because when you give you get.

## THE LESSON

☐ Unblur the lines between wants and needs.

☐ Learn to stay in your financial lane.

☐ Adopt a cash-only mentality if you can't control your spending when using cards.

☐ Reduce your credit card and overdraft limits so you can pay the total in one paycheck.

☐ Credit cards are not free money, so get rid of that free money mentality.

☐ Make money work for you.

☐ Start a side hustle.

☐ Secure an emergency fund.

## MORAL OF THE STORY

Your 20s is where you are hopeful and excited, with a promising future ahead. In order to set the foundation for financial success, take control of your finances early and start to make these vital decisions now. The earlier you start, the more of a habit it becomes, and this will set you up for financial success for many years to come.

CPSIA information can be obtained
at www.ICGtesting.com
Printed in the USA
LVHW090559031221
705100LV00002B/2